Anthony Ritthaler

Soaring
With
Eagles
Volume 2

A Book Of Freedom, Strength and Power

PUBLISHED by PARABLES
Earthly Stories with a Heavenly Meaning

ANTHONY RITTHALER

Pathways To The Past

Each volume stands alone as an Individual Book
Each volume stands together with others
to enhance the value of your collection

Build your Personal, Pastoral or Church Library
Pathways To The Past contains an ever-expanding list of
Christendom's most influencial authors

Augustine of Hippo
Athanasius
E. M. Bounds
John Bunyan
Brother Lawrence
Jessie Penn-Lewis
Bernard of Clairvaux
Andrew Murray
Watchman Nee
Arthur W. Pink
Hannah Whitall Smith
R. A. Torrey
A. W. Tozer
Jean-Pierre de Caussade
Thomas Watson
And many, many more.

Title: Soaring with Eagles Volume 2 A Book Of Freedom, Strength and Power
Anthony Ritthaler

Rights: All Rights Reserved
ISBN 978-1-945698-16-3
Doctrinal theology, Inspiration
Salvation, Meditation
Other books by this author include: Walking On The Water With Jesus (Volume 1 and 2), A Devil From The Beginning and Soaring With Eagles Volume 1

Anthony Ritthaler

Soaring With Eagles
Volume 2

A Book Of Freedom, Strength and Power

PUBLISHED *by* PARABLES
Earthly Stories with a Heavenly Meaning

Tony's Words Of Freedom, Strength and Power

ANTHONY RITTHALER

"The Devil is a liar,
but an Eagle just flies higher."

"When danger is all around
the Eagle takes off to higher ground."

"We have a choice as Christians:
we can hang with the crows, or soar with the pros."

"Your finest hour will always be
when you soar with God's Power."

"Fly with the Lord in Power, Strength, and Glory
and never allow Satan to write your life's story."

"When others around you complain and cry,
be mature take off and fly."

"Whenever you soar with God
this world will think your odd."

"When you are fighting the World, the flesh, and the Devil allow the Holy Spirit to move you to a higher level."

"The greatest person in life is not he who obtains the most, but it is he who is controlled by the blessed Holy Ghost."

"If you desire to be rare, that's when God can take you anywhere."

"Those who have the touch from on High will always give Satan a black eye."

"An Eagle often flies alone, but his journey leads to Gods Throne."

"When you're facing all the Demons of Hell, just fly to God and sing it is well."

"When like the Eagle you soar to the mountain, God will allow you to drink from His fountain."

"When an Eagle takes flight he never looks back, but that won't stop the Pharisees from taking smack."

Table of Contents

Tony's Words Of Freedom, Strength and Power
Table Of Contents
Special Thanks
Introduction

1. How Excellent is Thy Loving Kindness, Oh God!
2. How to Get Victory Over Depression
3. Three Things That Eagles Have That Christian's Need Desperately
4. The Power of a Good Testimony
5. Jesus Calmed My Storm on the Inside
6. Rejoice in the Lord Always, No Matter How Bad You Feel
7. A Friend Like No Other
8. The Stamp of Approval from Almighty God
9. If You Will Give God Your Little Lunch, He Can Multiply it for Years to Come
10. Feeling God's Angels All Around

11. Pay It Forward
12. Getting A Big Surprise While Driving Home One Night
13. Our God Knows What We Have Need Of
14. There's a Miracle in the Making
15. Jesus is Always There When We Need Him
16. The Lord Will Hear When I Call Upon Him
17. Call Unto Me and I Will Answer Thee
18. The Goodness of God Leadeth Thee to Repentance
19. But My God Shall Supply All Your Need
20. Amazing Grace, How Sweet the Sound
Conclusion

Special Thanks

I want to donate this special thanks portion to five special men that have been such an encouragement to me. Four of these men are radio hosts, and all five men practice what they preach. My respect and admiration for these men of God is hard to put into words and I hope through this section of the book you will seek to know them all yourself. Every one of these men are the real deal, and I'm honored that God has brought them my way and I thank Him every day for it. When I examine these men's lives, I see integrity, hard work, Godly charity, a vision for the lost, kindness, and faith. Let me list these five men and pay them the honor they so richly deserve.

The first man I would like to thank today is Bro Richard Frazier, host of The Richard Frazier Show on 760 Wurl Radio Moody Alabama. Bro Frazier has given his life to help other people's ministries and so many love this wonderful saint of God. You will be hard pressed to find a kinder Christian, and my respect for him is off the charts. Bro Frazier has had me on his show, he prays for me and my family, and he has been a true support to my ministry. Bro Frazier is one of these rare

Christians that walks with the fruit of the spirit and it shines through on a daily basis. Bro Frazier, thanks for being a friend, a support, a blessing, and a prayer warrior for me. May God continue to bless your ministry in many glorious way's.

The next man I would like to mention in my special thanks is Bro Bob Hill, host of Wbni Christian Radio. Bro Hill has truly humbled me by his financial support, his pure heart, and his support in passing my books to those in need. Nearly every day he blesses me with either a prayer, a word of advice, or a kind word from above. This world really needs more men like this and words on paper will never capture the blessing Bro Hill has been. Thank you my friend for your belief in my ministry and for being such an encouragement to me. Your friendship really touches my heart.

The third person I would like to praise for a moment is the great Nate Fortner, host of the Authors Minute and owner of Whosoever Press. Bro Fortner is a singer, an author, a business owner, a mentor, a friend, and a support to so many around this country. God sent Bro Fortner along my pathway at a time that was a blessing and my life has only become better through his influence upon my life. Folks, you need to look up Bro Fortner and get to know him on a personal level. Bro Nate Fortner is one of the most talented men in America and yet one of the most humble at the same time. Often, I find myself taking notes of how he conducts his life and I try to add these traits to mine as well. Bro Fortner, I want to thank you for all of your support through the years, and I pray great blessings on your life. You're a great man and I praise God for the example you set for a world that needs Jesus. Keep up the awesome work, I love you man of God.

The next man I want to thank is Bro Ken Mitchell, President of Missions Radio. When I think of character, faith, and dedication, Bro Mitchell comes to mind instantly. Every day of his life, Bro Mitchell goes out of his way to enrich someone else's life, and his heart is completely controlled by the Lord. The impact of his ministry is vast, and the rare gifts that he possesses are a blessing. Time and time again, Bro Mitchell has proven to be a friend, a servant, a giver, and a great testimony to those around him. Without men like Bro Mitchell, this world would be a far darker place. Bro Mitchell, I would not be where I am right now without your impact on my life. Thank you from the bottom of my heart for the blessing you have been over the last few years.

Last, but not least, I want to say a big thank you to my friend, Mr. John Jeffries, owner of Published By Parables Ministry. Bro Jeffries is my publisher, my friend, and one of my heroes in the faith. His constant help blesses me, and his old fashion character inspires me every day. Bro Jeffries has a heavy burden to reach the world and his outstanding heart helps him touch so many. Without Bro Jeffries help towards my ministry, we would not be where we are today. There is no way I could thank him enough for his support, his love, and his labor towards these books. Bro Jeffries, thanks for allowing my dreams to come true through your ministry, and thanks for being a man who I can look up to.

Folks, this world needs Christians like the five I just mentioned. Far too many use the Christian name for the wrong reasons, but these men make God smile. Thanks once again to all you men for being such a joy to know and an encouragement to this old sinner. God bless you all in a special way.

Introduction

Welcome to Volume Two of Soaring With Eagles; where once again the central theme will center around the great power of our Savior, Jesus Christ. Every story will bring honor to God above, and each story will motivate you to soar to higher ground. Churches around this country are filled with just average Christians who refuse to throw up the white flag of surrender and the cause of Christ suffers because of it. God wants us to be on fire for His glory; making a difference in a hopeless world. God expects His children to have a hunger to seek revival in their own personal life and I pray these stories will give you that desire.

As you read these stories, allow God to do a work in your heart. May the Holy Spirit of God speak to your heart as you read, and allow Him to change you from the inside out.

Sadly, when I go into churches in these last days, it's like I'm forced to watch an episode of the Walking Dead. People have no joy, they stagger around like zombies, spiritually speaking. They won't sing, they won't shout, they won't grow, they are half asleep, they have no direction, no drive, no purpose, and they make no impact for Christ. Folks, we need revival in our hearts again and a passion to reach the lost.

My prayer with this book is that these stories will charge you back up for God again, and cause you to thirst after His power. We serve a God that wants to show His power in all of our lives, but it will not happen unless we get serious again. Please enjoy the stories to come and allow God to transform you by His amazing grace.

Chapter One

How Excellent is Thy Loving Kindness, Oh God!

The God we serve is a God of tender compassion and loving kindness. If we have a desire to live for Him, he will honor us with things we desire and love. The Bible says in James 1:17, "Every good gift and every perfect gift is from above". Our Heavenly Father has a special place in His heart for those that put Him first in their life. The Bible says in Matthew 6:33 "Seek ye first the Kingdom of God, and His righteousness, and all these things shall be added unto you". When our children listen and obey us, we have a tendency to want to be a blessing in return because they make us proud. God in Heaven does the same thing for those that serve Him. The Bible says in Isaiah 1:19 "If ye be willing and obedient, ye shall eat the good of the land". We are serving a gracious and kind God who writes down all the good seeds we sow, and in His time he will reward us with things near and dear to our hearts. God knows our frame, he knows what we desire and he looks forward to blessing us in ways that are special to us. The Bible says in

Psalm 37:4 "Delight thyself also in the Lord; and he shall give thee the desires of thine heart". When our lives please God, we can expect great blessings to come our way because that is how God operates. The Bible says in Psalm 68:19 "Blessed be the Lord, who daily loadeth us with benefits". As we live life down here we should always be at peace knowing that God shelters us in the palm of his hand. The next story will show the world that God really cares for His own and will bless us if we put Him first.

One day, while working in Canton, Michigan, we passed a restaurant that I heard so much about but had never been to before. The restaurant was called IHOP, where they serve endless pancakes morning, noon, and night. The man I was working with couldn't believe I had never been there and he told me I needed to go as soon as possible. I remember looking at this man and saying, "Sir, if God wants me to go to IHOP he will reveal it unto me". Around two weeks later, a woman approached me at church with a gift for me and my wife, Erin. The woman looked at me and said "Tony, I thought you may like this, so enjoy". After we thanked this dear woman of God, we opened the gift and to our amazement it was a gift card for $250 to IHOP. God seen fit to make a way for us to enjoy this wonderful place and now Erin's Grandfather takes us every Sunday and refuses to let us pay. The Lord knows how to bless us in special ways and this was a blessing to me. We shall close out this chapter with Psalm 34:15 "The eyes of the Lord are upon the righteous, and His ears are open unto their cry".

Scriptures For This Chapter

Psalm 37:4 "Delight thyself also in the Lord; and He shall give thee the desires of thine heart."

Isaiah 1:19 "If ye be willing and obedient, ye shall eat the good of the land:"

Matthew 6:33 "But seek ye first the kingdom of God, and His righteousness: and all these things shall be added unto you."

Chapter 2

How to Get Victory Over Depression

In these last days of darkness, depression is sweeping through our land at an alarming rate. The Devil is having a field day with people's minds and millions are committing suicide because of it. In the Book of John, Ch. 10:10, the Bible declares "That the thief cometh not, but to steal, and to kill, and to destroy" and sadly this is happening all over this world. The Bible teaches us in I Peter 5:8 that the Devil, "As a roaring lion, walketh about, seeking whom he may devour". Folks, the Devil is on the warpath more now than he has ever been before because he knows his time is short. Satan is completely controlling people's minds in these last days and his ultimate goal is to keep us depressed and weak on a daily basis. Every single day of my life I talk to people in deep depression and it breaks my heart. The man in Mark Ch. 5 was possessed with around 6000 demons in one human body. Day in and day out this man remained in a hopeless state, crying and cutting himself with stones.

Satan sat back and laughed at this man's misery and he does the same with all mankind. If he can fill your heart and mind with his never ending lies, he will then keep you in his prison with no intentions of ever letting you out. The Bible says in II Timothy 2:26 that "The Devil takes people captive at his own will". In Luke 13 we read about a woman who was bound by Satan for 18 long, miserable years. Satan is the master deceiver and sadly he has a larger following than Jesus Christ. So many across this world make the mistake of allowing the devil to influence them and this decision results in total regret and misery. God has designed men to have peace, joy, love, and liberty but people would rather listen to lies more than truth and it bites them like an adder. Depression has risen at an incredible rate over the last 10 years and instead of running to the answer, people run to drugs, alcohol, parties, and doctors. People who run to these avenues of help usually come back far worse than they were before they went.

With the remainder of this chapter, I want to point you to the answer and it is the cure to all man's diseases and it has always been the formula for success so listen up. The key to victory always begins in one's head. The battle begins in the mind and Christ wants to capture your thoughts with glorious heavenly things. Satan, on the other hand, will flood our minds with doubt and questions that trouble our souls. Whenever you are overwhelmed with emotions and fear, leave Satan in the dust and run to Jesus as fast as you possibly can. The Bible says in I John 4:18 "That perfect love casteth out fear". The Word of God also tells us in Hebrews 2:14-15 that the lord came to "Deliver them who through fear of death were all their lifetime subject to bondage". The scriptures tell us in II Timothy 1:7 "That God hath not given us the spirit of fear; but of power, and of love, and of a sound mind". There is only one way to have joy unspeakable and full of glory and that is through the Lord, Jesus Christ. When the maniac lost all hope he made a great choice and ran to Jesus because he knew within his heart Christ was the only one who could break the chains of bondage in his life. The Bible records that after this choice was made, this crazy man was never the same again. The Bible clearly states in Mark Ch. 5:15 "And they come to Jesus, and see him that was possessed with the Devil, and had the legion sitting, and clothed, and in his right mind: and they were afraid".

There is good news my friends, no matter how low you feel, or how many mistakes you make, there is Hope through a forgiving God who longs to clean up our lives and minds through his blood. The Bible says in Isaiah 26:3 "Thou wilt keep him in perfect peace, whose mind is stated on thee: because he trusteth in thee. The Bible also says in Philippians 4:7 "And the peace of God, which passeth all understanding, shall keep your hearts and minds through Christ Jesus". The Word of God tells us in I Peter 1:13 "To gird up the lions of your mind" and in Philippians 2:5 the Lord says "Let this mind be in you which was also in Christ Jesus". The Bible declares that Jesus is the God of peace found in Romans 16:20, and that he the prince of peace in Isaiah 9:6. You see Satan can offer you cheap thrills and fun but it is impossible for him to offer peace and that's what the world needs more than anything else. Jesus is the only person who can offer abiding peace and He promises if we will draw nigh to him he will draw nigh to us. If you feed your spirit more than you feed your flesh, you will quickly start to gain victories in your life. God has never designed us to live defeated, sad, depressed, and confused, but rather he designed us to have peace, joy, freedom, and liberty through Christ. Always remember God is not the author of confusion and we will always offer help, mercy, pardon, forgiveness, and victory when we need answers. The Bible says in Luke 4:18 "The spirit of the Lord is upon me, because he hath anointed me to preach the gospel to the poor; He hath sent me to hear the broken-hearted, to preach deliverance to the captives, and recovering of sight to the blind, to set at liberty them that are bruised".

My friends, Jesus is willing and able to give you rest, don't delay; get to Jesus today. Refuse to allow Satan to deceive you any longer, submit to God's calling and you can be delivered from depression. Surround your life with Godly music, Godly people, and Godly preaching and it will guard you from the valleys of depression. Saturate yourself with God's word and allow His peace to invade your heart. Jesus is the answer and he can still bring out those which are bound with chains. The Bible declares in John 8:32 "And ye shall know the truth, and the truth shall set you free". Realize today that your only hope for everlasting joy and victory resides in Jesus, God's son. The Bible says in I Corinthians 15:57 "But thanks be to God, which giveth us the victory through our Lord Jesus Christ". The Word of God says in I John 5:4 "For whatsoever is born of God overcometh the world: and this is the victory that overcometh the world, even our faith". There is no pain you feel that He cannot heal. There is no storm that He cannot calm. There is no burden that He cannot lift. And there is no sin He cannot forgive. The Bible says in I John 1:9 "If we confess our sins, He is faithful and just to forgive us our sins, and to cleanse us from all unrighteousness". If you feel like you're going to drown from the waves of depression, reach out to Jesus and he will deliver you. The Bible says in Psalm 40:2 "He brought me up also out of a horrible pit, out of the miry clay, and set my feet upon a book, and established my goings". Jesus is the answer and if you need help, burdens are lifted at Calvary.

Scriptures For This Chapter

Psalm 40:2 "He brought me up also out of a horrible pit, out of a miry clay, and set my feet upon a rock, and established my goings."

Isaiah 9:6 "For unto us a child is born, unto us a son is given: and the government shall be upon His shoulder: and His name shall be called wonderful, counselor, the Mighty God, the everlasting Father, the Prince of Peace."

Isaiah 26:3 "Thou wilt keep him in perfect peace, whose mind is stayed on thee: because he trusteth in thee."

Mark 5:15 "And they come to Jesus, and see him that was possessed with the Devil, and had the legion, sitting, and clothed, and in his right mind: and they were afraid."

Luke 13:16 "And ought not this woman, being a daughter of Abraham, whom Satan hath bound, lo, these eighteen years, be loosed from this bond on the Sabbath Day?"

John 8:32 "And ye shall know the truth, and the truth shall make you free."

II Timothy 2:26 "And that they may recover themselves out of the snare of the devil, who are taken captive by him at his will."

James 4:7 "Submit yourselves therefore to God. Resist the Devil, and he will flee from you."

I Peter 1:8 "Whom having not seen, ye love; in whom, though now ye see Him not, yet believing, ye rejoice with joy unspeakable and full of glory."

I Peter 1:13 "Wherefore gird up the loins of your mind, be sober, and hope to the end for the grace that is to be brought unto you at the revelation of Jesus Christ."

I John 1:9 "If we confess our sins, He is faithful and just to forgive us our sins, and to cleanse us from all unrighteousness."

Chapter 3

Three Things That Eagles Have That Christian's Need Desperately

If you have never done a deep study about eagles and their many special gifts, you are really missing out. Everything about the eagle is remarkable and they have always represented liberty, freedom, power, and conquerors.

God designed them to be unique and rare and the Bible describes them as very special. We as Christians should all take notes of the many unique qualities of eagles and we should do our best to add them to our lives. There are not very many Christians that are soaring with God anymore, and it is killing revival in our churches. In days gone by so many saints of God excelled like the eagle in so many areas. But, my friends, it's not the same anymore. Christians are now content with being lukewarm in these last days and this wicked mindset literally makes God sick. With the remainder of this chapter I want to highlight three amazing traits that eagles possess and I pray to

God that we develop a desire to add them to our life. May we all have a great desire to soar like the eagle all the days of our life.

The first thing that I would like to point out that the eagle has that we desperately need is great vision. It is said that an eagle can see at least ten times farther than humans can. God has designed an eagle's eye to see things coming from miles away and this gift allows them to react quicker, hunt better, and accomplish far more because of keen awareness. Folks in church are content with being average and we have totally lost our vision for a lost world dying and going to Hell. The Bible says in Proverbs 29:18 "Where there is no vision the people perish". The eagle uses its eyesight as a great advantage and it allows them to gain an edge over his enemies.

The Bible describes the last day church as wretched, and miserable, and poor, and blind, and naked. The Eagle wins many battles and is a victor in nearly everything it does, while most saints I know just struggle to get out of bed each morning. Christians, we need to open our eyes to the reality that people need the Lord and the world needs us to have a vision like Jesus again.

The Devil has literally rocked the church to sleep and it's high time that we awake out of our dead condition. The eagle is always prepared through its great vision and that's why they are respected like no other bird that exists. Christians, we need to beg God for the vision to make a difference in a crooked and perverse generation.

Allow God to give you a supernatural vision like the

eagle to reach a dark world in need of Christ. If we seek after a great vision, our churches could see revival once again.

The second thing the eagle has that Christians really need is great strength. An eagle has ten times the grip pressure humans do and they are feared by all. We as Christians are expected and commanded to be strong in the Lord. The Book of Ephesians 6:10 says this "Finally, my brethren, be strong in the Lord, and in the power of His might". We are commanded to walk in the fruit of the spirit while putting on the whole armor of God. The Bible says in Isaiah 40:31 that an eagle will constantly renew their strength year in and year out and they can soar to heights unknown. The Bible commands Christians to get stronger as time goes on and to grow in His grace. Most Christians are either going backwards or staying neutral and the Devil beats them up. We need more David's who have a power from another world and are not afraid to step up to their Goliath's. We need more Sampson's, Joshua's, and Gideon's who fear God, not man. So many Christians walk around defeated, weak, helpless, and powerless, as the Devil slaps them around. We as Christians are meant to experience victories, triumphs, and blessings as we grow stronger in the Lord every day. The Bible says in Romans 8:31 "What shall we then say to these things? If God be for us, who can be against us?" The Word of God also says this in II Corinthians 2:14 "Now thanks be unto God which always causeth us to triumph in Christ".

There is nothing more amazing than an eagle in flight, and most Christians will only watch in wonder because of their refusal to be strong Christians. God wants us to get stronger day in and day out and without this quality in our lives we will never win battles over the enemy. Allow God to fill you with His power and strength and your life will begin to take off.

The last thing that an eagle has that Christians need is a spirit that is in submission to the wind. It is very clear throughout God's word that the wind is a type of the Holy Ghost and an eagle will allow the wind to carry him where he needs to go. For the majority of the eagle's life he will use the strength of the wind and not his own and this is why he is so successful. We as Christians need to really take note of this. Christians are dropping out of God's will at a record pace because they are doing things in their own strength without God's spirit. The Bible clearly declares in Philippians 4:13 that "I can do all things through Christ which strengtheneth me". When we rely on God's unending strength and ability rather than our own, the results are staggering. Far too often as we travel through this life we make the mistake of trusting in our own ability and we grow weary very quickly. Christians are falling over and over because they are not allowing God to control them and use them for His honor and glory. The Book of Galatians says "This I say then, walk in the spirit, and ye shall not fulfill the lusts of the flesh". An eagle remains fresh, strong, and victorious all because he yields to the wind for the longevity of his life. In the Book of John 15:5 Jesus said "For without me ye can do nothing". Without the power of the Holy Ghost controlling our lives on a regular basis, the end result will always be failure. The eagle is showing us by example that we can never soar to new heights without the influence of the wind from another world. Never operate in your own strength, learn how the eagle conducts itself and add these three qualities to your life. The eagle is the king of the air and if we want to fly with the Lord we must have a vision for the lost, great strength of the Lord, and a total submission to the wind from above.

Let's close this chapter with this power verse and I pray this verse will be the testimony of all our lives. II Samuel 1:23 "Saul and Jonathan were lovely and pleasant in their lives, and in their death they were not divided: they were swifter than eagles, they were stronger than lions".

Scriptures For This Chapter

II Samuel 1:23 "Saul and Jonathan were lovely and pleasant in their lives, and in their death they were not divided: they were swifter than eagles, they were stronger than lions."

Proverbs 29:18 "Where there is no vision, the people perish: but he that keepeth the law, happy is he."

Isaiah 40:31 "But they that wait upon the Lord shall renew their strength; they shall mount up with wings as eagles; they shall run, and not be weary; and they walk, and not faint."

John 15:5 "I am the vine, ye are the branches: he that abideth in me, and I in him, the same bringeth forth much fruit: for without me ye can do nothing."

Romans 8:31 "What shall we then say to these things? If God be for us, who can be against us?"

II Corinthians 2:14 "Now thanks be unto God, which always causeth us to triumph in Christ, and maketh manifest the savior of His knowledge by us in every place."

Galatians 5:16 "This I say then, walk in the spirit, and ye shall not fulfill the lusts of the flesh."

Ephesians 6:10 "Finally, my brethren, be strong in the Lord, and in the power of His might."

Philippians 4:13 "I can do all things through Christ which strengtheneth me."

Chapter 4

The Power of a Good Testimony

There is nothing in this world that carries more value with God like a good testimony does. The Bible says in Psalm Ch. 4:3 "But know that the Lord hath set apart him that is godly for himself". There is no denying the fact that Joseph, Joshua, Daniel, John the Baptist, Elijah, and others like them had an extra special influence and annoitting than the average Christian did in their day. God wants us to be holy as He is holy and in this day the way His children live breaks His heart. Christians seem to forget that the Lord of glory watches our lives and records our works in a book. This thought alone should cause His children to have a desire to walk the straight and narrow, but sadly, many don't even care.

My Dad did a wonderful job to instill in me as a young boy the fear of the Lord and the importance of a good testimony. Ever since I've been a little boy, I've been extremely careful of what I say, what I do, and where I go. The Bible says in Proverbs 1:7 "The fear of the Lord is the beginning of knowledge: but fools despise wisdom and instruction". As I live my life, I fully understand that I do not have the power to live other's lives for them, but I do have the power to walk in a way that pleases God. The Bible teaches in Colossians 1:10 "That we should walk worthy of the Lord unto all pleasing, being fruitful in every good work, and increasing in the knowledge of God. Paul begs Christians in Romans 12:1 "To present their bodies as a living sacrifice, holy, acceptable unto God, which is your responsible service". The Bible commands us to live in a way that is pleasing to God and as a result we will be a sweet fragrance in the nostrils of God. The Bible says in Philippians Ch. 2:15 "That we may be blameless and harmless, the sons of God, without rebuke, in the midst of a crooked and a perverse nation, among whom ye shine as lights in the world". Jesus commanded us in Matthew Ch. 5:16 "To let our light so shine before men, that they may see your good works, and glorify your father which is in Heaven". In my entire life I can only remember saying one curse word at the age of five. Never in my life have I drank a beer, been to a worldly party, smoked cigarettes, done drugs, or hung out with the evil crowd. Can you give that kind of testimony?

The Book of Psalm Ch. 1:1 says this "Blessed is the man that walketh not in the council of the ungodly, nor standeth in the ways of sinners, not sitteth in the seat of the scornful". But his delight is in the law of the Lord; and in his law doth he meditate day and night. God desires and expects us all to bring honor to His precious son and we cannot accomplish this if we buddy up with Satan most of the week. Jesus himself said this in Matthew 6:24 "No man can serve two masters". God wants us to serve him with every single fiber of our being. The

Bible says this in mark 12:30 "And thou shalt love the Lord thy God with all thy heart, with all thy soul, with all thy mind, and with all thy strength: this is the first commandment". Far too many Christians try to live in the world throughout the week and then play the part as Christian on Sundays. This kind of lifestyle literally makes God sick, and He clarifies this in Revelation Ch. 3:16 "Without living pure and clean before the Lord we will never reach our full potential". Every day as we get out of bed in the morning we should make a clear choice to die to self and serve the Savior. The Bible says this in Matthew 16:24 "Then said Jesus unto His disciples, if any man will come after me, let him deny himself, and take up his cross, and follow me". How important is your testimony to you? People are constantly watching our lives and they are just waiting for us to stumble. When Jesus ministered during His time on earth literally thousands of lost and religious people hung on every word not to learn but to only find fault. My greatest fear in life is to make a major mistake that will bring a reproach to the Lord Almighty. The pressure to walk on the water is heavy but it is not heavier than the cross our Lord carried. We all should do our part to be a light that shines forth to a dark world. The Bible tells us in Proverbs 4:18 "But the path of the just is as a shining light, that shineth more and more unto the perfect day". Let me ask you a question; are you shining more and more every day? Does the world see a difference in your life? We owe it to the Lord to be that light that He commands us to be. When people saw Elijah coming they stopped and took notice because they knew he had a testimony second to none. When you show up on the scene do people sense this about you? Every one of us should take our walk with the Lord seriously and I fear in these days it's not important like it should be. As long as people live half-hearted, people will remain hopeless and destitute of peace because we are dropping the ball. People depend on us to be an example that they can learn from. Are you comparable to a David, a Jeremiah, a Stephen, or a Moses? Sadly, most can be compared to a Lot or Judas. What kind of testimony do you possess?

As I close out this chapter I want to share a blessing with you that cheered my heart concerning my testimony. On Facebook they had a link posted where people could go on there and see who they're comparable to from the Bible. The comparison is computed due to ones way of life, and testimony as a whole. I submitted my profile and Facebook compared me to John the Baptist and the Angel Gabriel. Although I know I'm not even close, it blessed me beyond measure. I'm wondering as we close the page on this chapter who would you be compared to if you submitted your information? Live right everyone, God takes it very serious, I promise.

Scriptures For This Chapter

Psalm 4:3 "But know that they Lord hath set apart him that is Godly for himself: the Lord will hear when I call unto Him."

Psalm 1:1 "Blessed is the man that walketh not in the council of the ungodly, nor standeth in the way of sinners, nor sitteth in the seat of the scornful."

Proverbs 1:7 "The fear of the Lord is the beginning of knowledge: but fools despise wisdom and instruction."

Proverbs 4:18 "But the path of the just is as a shining light, that shineth more and more unto the perfect day."

Matthew 5:16 "Let your light so shine before men, that they may see your good works, and glorify your father which is in Heaven."

Matthew 7:13 "Enter ye in at the straight gate: for wide is the gate, and broad is the way, that leadeth to destruction, and many there be which go in thereat."

Matthew 6:24 "No man can serve two masters: for either he will hate the one, and love the other: or else he will hold to the one, and despise the other, ye cannot serve God and mammon."

Matthew 16:24 "Then said Jesus unto His disciples, if any man will come after me, let him deny himself, and take up his cross, and follow me."

Mark 12:30 "And thou shalt love the Lord thy God with all thy heart, and with all thy soul, and with all thy mind, and with all thy strength; this is the first commandment."

Romans 12:1 "I beseech you therefore, brethren, by the mercies of God, that ye present your bodies a living sacrifice, holy, acceptable unto God which is your reasonable service."

Philippians 2:15 "That ye may be blameless and harmless, the sons of God, without rebuke, in the midst of a crooked and perverse nation, among whom ye shine as lights in the world."

Colossians 1:10 "That ye might walk worthy of the Lord unto all pleasing, being fruitful in every good work, and increasing in the knowledge of God."

I Peter 1:16 "Because it is written, be ye holy; for I am holy."

Revelation 3:16 "So then because thou art lukewarm, and neither cold nor hot, I will spew thee out of my mouth."

CHAPTER 5

JESUS CALMED MY STORM ON THE INSIDE

Jesus has the ability to calm every storm that comes our way, but we must believe he can. So many Christians are sinking in the pit of doubt, but Jesus wants to set them on a solid rock by His marvelous grace. When is the last time you heard God's voice? If it's been a long time, may I suggest you lighten the load of noise surrounding your life and open your ears to that still small voice. Too many people in these last days are stressed to the max, and they are ready to explode at any second. Christians do not seem to have the ability to hear God's voice anymore and it's leading them astray. We as saints of God should all be in a position to hear His voice, and if we can't it's our fault, not God's. Whenever our spirit is troubled, we can go to the rock of ages and find relief. Sometimes our hearts and minds race and we find ourselves feeling overcharged with the cares of this life. The Devil wants us to rush, go fast, and worry about everything. God wants us to slow down, wait on Him, and be at peace. Sometimes in this fast moving society, we as Christians must learn to slow down, calm our emotions, and listen for His voice. The next story is a wonderful story that will bless your soul. Allow God to help you as you take in this blessed story.

One morning I woke up to reports that the weather was turning bad and there was a 100% chance of rain. The news also said that rain would start at around 7:30 A.M. and last until 3:00 P.M. When I heard this news, it troubled me because the homecoming football game was on this exact day and the lines for the field had to be perfect, so I began to worry. When I arrived at 7:00 A.M. that morning, the sky looked pitch black so I felt naturally rushed. When I went into the building I quickly grabbed the painter and the things I needed and hurried to the field to paint the football lines for the big game. The sky grew darker and darker and I was working at a high speed to beat the rain. My soul was troubled and my emotions were getting out of control and I had no clue how I would get the field done in time. Moments after these thoughts rushed through my mind I felt a peace from above saying "turn the machine down and take your time, it will not rain until you're finished with your work". After feeling this peace, I followed the Lord's voice and turned the machine to its slowest level and had total confidence that God spoke to me. I'll never forget the instant change of emotions that day and I had not one fear that it would rain until the job was complete. Instead of being stressed, I began to sing, and worship God right there on the field. When I finished the field it was 9:00 A.M. and the sky looked like something from a horror film but still no rain. On my way back to park the painter in the shed I kept the painter on slow and stopped to talk to a man named John for around 10 minutes. Once this was over, I did another job that lasted around 15 minutes and then I started to head towards the shop. On my way back I saw a woman rushing to throw trash away so I stopped to give her a hand. The woman looked at me and said "rain is coming, find shelter". When she said this I told her "once I park this painter in the shed the rain will come, but not until then". Around 3 minutes later I arrived in the shed and rain pounded the building. God held off the rain that day and Huron High won their game.

The Lord wants us to trust His word, not our emotions. When Jesus whispers peace be still all storms must obey. The Bible says this in Psalm 86:10 "For thou art great, and doest wondrous things, thou art God alone". When I look back at what God did that day I stand in awe and praise his Holy name. The Bible says in Psalm 83:18 "That men may know that thou, whose name alone is JEHOVAH, art the most high over all the earth". God wants His children to trust in His ability, not our own. If we keep this in mind our worry and fear will begin to disappear. Praise god for His power that can still any storm.

Scriptures For This Chapter

Psalm 83:18 "That men may know that thou, whose name alone is JEHOVAH, art the most high over all the earth."

Psalm 86:10 "For thou art great, and doest wondrous things: thou art God alone."

Mark 4:39 "And He arose, and rebuked the wind, and said unto the sea, peace be still. And the wind ceased, and there was a great calm."

Chapter 6

Rejoice in the Lord Always, No Matter How Bad You Feel

The Word of God says in Philippians 4:4 "Rejoice in the Lord always: and again I say rejoice". When Paul penned down this wonderful verse he was writing from prison and the conditions were miserable. In Acts ch 16 we find this Paul fella once again bound in prison, singing and praising God along with Silas and enjoying the spirit of the Lord. The great Apostle Paul was showing us through his writing and through the life he lived that Christians can worship no matter what state they find themselves in. The next time you are going through a trail of a storm just start singing and praising the Lord and see what happens. Christians need to learn that God is good all the time and He is worthy to be praised. All throughout the Word of God we find God blessing those that praised Him through the fire. Always remember you cannot be down and rejoice at the same time. Praising the Lord drives away doubt and fear and ushers in the joy of the Lord. The Bible says the joy of the Lord is our strength and God wants us to be strong during the dark times of life. Whenever we are mature enough to worship through our sad times, God will show up and bless us in special ways. The Bible teaches in Psalm 147:3 that God "Healeth the broken in heart, and bindeth up their wounds". Always understand in your heart that no matter how alone you feel God loves you and wants to comfort you. Allow Him to comfort you through worship and the results will be a blessing. Whenever I feel down in the valley I make it a habit to praise His name and when I do the blessings of the Lord always seem to flow. The next story is just an example of the importance of praising God no matter how we feel and the reward that comes because of it. Allow this story to bless your heart.

One morning as I was driving to work I made the mistake of having a pity party and focusing on my storm more than the Savior. The Devil filled my soul with sadness and depression started setting in. My mind was dwelling on the wrong things and I knew I had to turn my focus back on Jesus so I turned on a Gospel CD and began to worship. Almost instantly I sensed God's presence enter my car and I put both hands in the air and rejoiced in His goodness. My heart was revived and I thanked God over and over for His blessings and His mercy upon my life. When I got to work I received a call from a woman who had been praying for my book ministry. She said "Tony, just a few minutes ago you came to my mind and I felt led by God to give you $200 for your ministry". When I looked at my watch I noticed it was around the same time I was praising God through my storms. Always worship God despite how you feel and God will smile down upon you. If you're in the valley encourage yourself in the Lord and God may show up. The Bible says in Psalm 145:2 "Every day will I bless thee, and I will praise thy name forever and ever". Rise up out of the ashes and cry out from your soul "The Lord giveth and the Lord taketh away blessed be the name of the Lord". Worthy is the lamb who was slain.

Scriptures For This Chapter

Psalm 145:2 "Every day will I bless thee: and I will bless thy name for ever and ever."

Psalm 147:3 "He healeth the broken in heart, and bindeth up their wounds."

Job 1:21 "And said, naked came I out of my mother's womb, and naked shall I return thither: the Lord gave, and the Lord hath taken away; blessed be the name of the Lord."

Acts 16:25 "And at midnight Paul and Silas prayed, and sang praises unto God: and the prisoners heard them."

Philippians 4:4 "rejoice in the Lord always: and again I say, rejoice."

Chapter 7

A Friend Like No Other

There is a friend that sticketh closer than a brother and his name is Jesus Christ. So many different people we meet will tell us that they will never leave us and even die for us but when the hard times arrive you can't find those people with the FBI. Folks, there is no man who keeps his word quite like Jesus does. Hebrews 13:5 "Promises that He will never leave us nor forsake us" and throughout the ages of times this has proven to be true in the lives of countless believers. The Bible tells us in John 15:13 "That there is no greater love than this that a man lay down his life for his friends". The Lord proved His love for each and every one of us on a bloody hillside called Calvary, and the Bible teaches that we owe Him everything. The Bible says in Proverbs 17:17 that "a friend loveth at all times" and whenever I think upon this verse I immediately think about our Lord and Savior, Jesus Christ. The great old song describes Him like this "The God of the mountain is still God in the valley". No matter how hard this life becomes we have assurance from the Word of God that we will never walk alone. The great hymn writer penned these wonderful words from the depths of his heart "What a friend we have in Jesus, all our sins and griefs to bear, and what a privilege to carry everything to God in prayer". Whatever pain we feel, no matter what storm comes our way, nothing is too big for Jesus. God loves us with an everlasting love that is beyond human comprehension and he longs to have fellowship with us. The Bible says in I John 1:7 "But if we walk in the light, as He is in the light, we have fellowship one with another, and the blood of Jesus Christ His son cleanseth us from all sins". Many Christians are burdened down with the many care's of life and it's hard to watch them struggle on a daily basis. Jesus offers relief and he stands at the hearts door of man just hoping for that door to swing open wide. The Bible says in Matthew 11:28 "Come unto me all, all ye that labor and are heavy laden, and I will give you rest". We as humans need to give up and let Jesus take over so we can have peace on the inside. Every single day we should have a desire to walk with the master and seek His will. Jesus wants to show us His power through a life yielded to Him. The Lord wants to walk with us and talk with us throughout our time on planet Earth. We should all be able to get a hold of God at any given time and that will never happen if we don't take our walk with Him seriously. We should tell the Lord often how much we love Him, and we should worship Him as much as possible. Whenever we walk close to Jesus, great things will come our way. May this next story capture the importance of walking ever so close to the Savior. I pray this story is a blessing to your soul.

Early one morning, as I was working at the school, I began telling the Lord how much I appreciate and love Him and I could feel His presence close by me. After a few minutes of singing and worshipping His most holy name, a verse came to my mind and it was a blessing on that cold Monday morning. The Lord directed me to I John 5:14 and this is what it says "And this is the confidence that we have in Him, that if we ask anything according to His will, He heareth us". For the next several minutes my heart and mind dwelt upon this verse and a prayer came to my lips. When my meditation was complete I began to pray to the Lord and beseech Him to answer this prayer from my heart. My prayer to God was simply this "Lord, I know you love me and I love you, I'm asking you right now to place it on someone's heart to give me exactly $100 and I will use it for your will".

When this prayer was over I went back to work with total confidence that God would answer this prayer. As the day unfolded, nothing seemed to happen but I had absolute faith this prayer would come to pass. Praise the Lord, later on that night the prayer came alive and it was a blessing to my soul. As we were going out of the church a man stopped us and said that the Lord placed it upon his heart to give us $100 and he prayed it would be of help. Folks, as I held that $100 the joy bells started ringing in my soul and once again I was praising His precious name. The Word of God tells us this in Psalm 34:15 "The eyes of the Lord are upon the righteous, and His ears are open unto their cry". Christians all across this world are missing out on His power and His blessings because they value something in this life more than their relationship with Jesus.

We will never experience joy unspeakable and full of glory again until we hunger and thirst for a relationship with Him. The old song says it like this "Though I fail the Lord, He has never failed me". This life at its best is sinking sand, but a wise man buildeth his house upon a rock. If you trust in the Lord He will never let you down. What a great friend we have in Jesus.

Scriptures For This Chapter

Psalm 34:15 "The eyes of the Lord are upon the righteous, and His ears are open to their cry."

Proverbs 17:17 "A friend loveth at all times, and a brother is born for adversity."

Jeremiah 31:3 "The Lord hath appeared of old unto me, saying, yea, I have loved thee with an everlasting love: therefore with loving kindness have I drawn thee."

John 15:13 "Greater love hath no man than this; that a man lay down His life for His friends."

Matthew 7:24 "Therefore whosoever heareth these sayings of mine, and doeth them, I will liken him unto a wise man, which built his house upon a rock."

Hebrews 13:5 "Let your conversation be without covetousness: and be content with such things as he have: for he hath said, I will never leave thee, nor forsake thee."

I John 1:7 "But if we walk in the light, as He is in the light, we have fellowship one with another, and the blood of Jesus Christ His Son cleanseth us from all sin."

I John 5:14 "And this is the confidence that we have in Him, that if we ask anything according to His will, He heareth us."

Chapter 8

The Stamp of Approval from Almighty God

If you are facing an important decision your life, please do yourself a favor and wait for direction from Almighty God. Whether you are going to preach a message, or produce a CD, or write a book, or anything else that requires a lot of work, sit down at the feet of Jesus and seek His will in your life. Whenever we try to make things come to pass on our own we will find it failing in a tragic way. Learn how to seek the council of the Lord and make sure His stamp of approval is applied to each and every decision you make. The Bible says this in Isaiah 9:6 "For unto us a child is born, unto us a son is given: and the government shall be upon His shoulder: and His name shall be called wonderful, counselor, the mighty God, the everlasting father, the prince of peace". Without asking council from our everlasting father, every decision we make will be void of peace. Seek His face early and often and wait on His guidance for however long it takes before jumping into a project. Always avoid being in a hurry when making decisions and always ask the Lord if it's His will before doing anything.

The Bible teaches in Psalm 37:23 "The steps of a good man are ordered by the Lord: and he delighteth in his way". Please make sure it's God's will, not yours, and strive to please Him and not your own fleshly desires. We need more ministries directed by Almighty God, and we need far less ministries that operate without the touch of the Lord. The story I will now give is powerful, and a real blessing to this old sinner boy. It's so wonderful to have a ministry directed by God and I'm sure after you read this story you will agree that God is in it. Allow God to bless you through this next story.

Around two years ago the Lord placed a strong burden on my heart to produce a second volume to the book Walking On The Water With Jesus. This burden was strong so I wanted to make sure it was the Lord dealing with me and not my own self ambitions, so I sought out to gain direction from on high. Quickly, I grabbed my Bible, my notes, and a copy of Walking On The Water With Jesus and I went to the back of the house to pray and meditate on this important decision. When I went in the back, I noticed my daughter left the TV on and it happened to be on the Discovery Channel so I just left it on. I remember looking up into Heaven and saying "Lord, if you want me to produce Walking On The Water With Jesus Volume 2, make it very clear to me right now". Immediately after I prayed this prayer I happened to look up at the TV and like a flash of lightening a lizard took off and was running on the water. When this happened it stunned me so I watched for a few minutes to make sure what I just witnessed was real. Sure enough, they were doing a special on a lizard that had the ability to walk on the water and this special lizard is commonly referred to as the Jesus lizard. Never in my life have I seen this lizard before but as I was praying for direction of God he allowed it to go across my TV set. As I viewed this lizard it seemed to run with so much freedom and at the moment the Lord told me to write the book with His approval so we submitted to His will. Folks, ever since this day the Lord has blessed this decision and so many have been touched by that book. It's amazing how God reveals things unto men when we seek His will above anything else. When you have a ministry with God's approval, great things are bound to happen. I'll never forget the power of this moment, and the joy I felt in my heart. We all need to sit at the feet of Jesus and seek His will in every situation we encounter. Let me close out the chapter with this verse Psalm 27:14 "Wait on the Lord: be of good courage, and He shall strengthen thine heart: wait, I say, on the Lord".

Scriptures For This Chapter

Psalm 27:14 "Wait on the Lord: be of good courage, and He shall strengthen thine heart: wait, I say, on the Lord."

Psalm 37:23 "The steps of a good man are ordered by the Lord: and he delighteth in his way."

Chapter 9

If You Will Give God Your Little Lunch, He Can Multiply It For Years To Come

How many times over the years has God directly spoken to us about giving up what we have to help the cause of Christ? If I were to ask for a show of hands on this question, I'm sure all of us could raise our hands and remember times when God pleaded with us about sacrificing for the greater good. God is pleased with those who listen to His voice, not those that ignore it. In the eyes of God, giving is a priceless act and He longs to use your gift of faith to further His wonderful plan in reaching others.

At different times in all of our lives, God tests us to see who will give and who will not. Those who obey receive great blessings and they who refuse fail the test. The Bible says in Matthew 17:20 "If ye have faith as a grain of a mustard seed, ye shall say unto this mountain, remove hence to yonder place;

and it shall remove". God is looking to do great miracles in our life but He is waiting for us to act by faith. In John Ch. 6:9 a boy was willing to give up his little lunch at God's command and as a result, around 25,000 were fed. The most amazing thing about this story is the fact that while the crowd was doubting, the lad was trusting and God performed a supernatural miracle. Jesus is looking for those who will give their little lunch, and when they do, blessings can flow for years to come. The Lord can take your gift of faith and multiply it in ways you have never dreamed. For the rest of this chapter I will list three different times God led me to give my little lunch and because I listened, many were blessed. Allow these three stories to motivate you to do the same.

While serving God in Detroit under the ministry of Dr. Lawrence Mendez, God seemed to move on me in every service. The need in Detroit was great, and the preaching was from the glory world. These two elements together pushed me to limits with God that I've never been before. Over and over again God would say "Give" and I would say "Yes, Lord". One night under Holy Ghost conviction, God spoke to me about buying the church a few buses so without question I acted on faith and gave up my lunch. Little did I know that night that God would allow those two buses to pick up thousands of kids for church for the next 15 years. Jesus took that little lunch and fed the multitudes with it and I give Him all the glory.

Another time God took my lunch and fed other was on a visitation night in Detroit. As we were knocking doors one night I overheard a dear lady mentioning that she needed a car or she would not be able to come to church anymore. Without hesitation, I took my check book out and with a heart of faith wrote her a check so she could get a car. This decision not only blessed me, but more importantly it blessed her and her family. She used the money to buy an old beat up car in hopes that it would last a year. My friends, God put His hand on that car and allowed her to bring her family to church for the next 11 years. If I would have not given up my little lunch that day, this woman's life may have ended up very differently. Always do what God tells you and you will never regret it.

The final story I will give concerning this subtext is amazing to say the least. Years ago, a dear preacher had a need for a used floor buffer for his hardwood floor business, so I felt led to get it for him. When I got him the machine it was old and used up but I asked God to allow it to be a blessing for years to come. Not long ago I asked this man of God if he still had the floor buffer. To my amazement he said "I still do and for 18 years I've never had one single problem with it". The preached told me that every morning as he looks at it he remembers my act of kindness and marvels how it lasted so long.

These are just three examples of what God can do if we are willing to give up our lunch for the cause of Christ. God wants to take our gift of faith and feed the world many times over. Just do what God commands and the blessings will last a lifetime. Allow God to do miracles through your life of faith and years down the road you will never regret it.

Scriptures For This Chapter

John 6:9 "There is a lad here, which hath five barley loaves, and two small fishes: but what are they among so many?"

Matthew 17:20 "And Jesus said unto them, because of your unbelief: verily I say unto you, if ye have faith as a grain of a mustard seed, ye shall say unto this mountain, remove hence to yonder place; and it shall remove; and nothing shall be impossible unto you."

Hebrews 11:6 "But without faith it is impossible to please Him: for he that cometh to God must believe that He is, and that He is a rewarder of them that diligently seek Him."

Chapter 10

Feeling God's Angels All Around

I've come to realize more and more as I get older that the angels of God are all around us. There are so many stories throughout the pages of time that reveal to us the powerful encounters of angels showing up on the scene when people needed them most. Seemly, every day I hear a story, or read about angels visiting mankind and it's hard to explain away. Many times throughout my own personal walk with God I've been humbled to sense the presence of angels around me. God has protected and sheltered me and my family on several occasions and we give Him the glory for that. We could probably all tell stories of the mercies of God concerning angels, and the Bible is filled with accounts as well. The following story is powerful, and I pray it will richly bless your heart.

Not long ago, we as a family took a trip to Pigeon Forge, Tennessee, and we had a blast. The trip lasted a week and we had many wonderful moments. As we were packing up to leave the Lord impressed on my heart to pray for safety on our way home so I did just that. My prayer to God was very simple and I asked for Him to send an angel to watch over us as we travelled home. Shortly into our journey back home, a car began to move into our lane and it just kept coming. I remember looking over and watching something hold back that car from completely coming into our lane. Folks, it was a miracle of God that we were not in an accident and I know an angel kept us safe. Around an hour later, we had another close call and we could sense His presence all around, keeping us safe. I often wonder what would have happened if I didn't pray. It is very possible that we would not be here today. The Bible says in Psalm 34:7 "The angel of the Lord encampeth round about them that fear Him, and delivereth Him". Thank God for the many angels that surround us that we cannot see. If God would open our spiritual eyes to how many were near us at any given time it would blow our minds. The Bible says in Hebrews 12:22 that there is an innumerable company of angels. There is no way of knowing how many angels exist today, we are just thankful God sent one to protect us that day. Thank God for His love and watch care over His children, we should never take that for granted.

Scriptures For This Chapter

Psalm 34:7 "The angel of the Lord encampeth round about them that fear Him, and delivereth them."

Hebrews 12:22 "But ye are come unto Mount Zion, and unto the city of the living God, the heavenly Jerusalem, and to an innumerable company of angels."

Chapter 11

Pay It Forward

How often have we all heard this saying "pay it forward"? Nearly every day I hear this saying by somebody, somewhere. The phrase "pay it forward" is basically taken from the Biblical principal of giving and receiving. Seemly, every human has their own wonderful story about how they gave to someone else and God returned a similar blessing later on for them. Folks, I'm no different and I too have a lot of great stories concerning this topic. The Word of God is filled with stories that bless our hearts and that prove that giving and receiving is a powerful thing. People are passionate about paying it forward because there is nothing more powerful than real stories that move the heart. My advice to all mankind is simply this: pay it forward to others and I promise it will come back to you. The Bible says in Ecclesiastes 11:1 "Cast thy bread upon the waters: for thou shalt find it after many days". When the Bible makes statements like this I promise you can go to sleep every night with confidence that it's true. The following story is a blessing and I hope it's a motivation for you to pay it forward every chance you get.

One day while coming out of Taco Bell, the Lord moved on my heart to dump out all my change on the ground to help someone in need. It seemed a bit unusual, but I knew the Lord spoke to me so I emptied out $2.52 on the ground next to my car. The man I was with said to me "what in the world are you doing, are you crazy?" When he said this, I said to him "yes, maybe, but God wants me to pay it forward and He told me to do it". The man said "Are you sure?" and I said "Yes, sir, I am, and I promise He will give it back and much more". The very next day, I was asked by my boss to work a Saturday and that rarely ever happens. As I walked into work the next morning, I could not believe my eyes. My job that day was to pick up trash all around the football field. God allowed me to pick up 38 dollars' worth of pop bottles in one afternoon. He also allowed me to work 3 hours overtime and I found three dollar bills as well. My mind kept flashing back to the day before when God led me to drop my change on the ground with the promise of it coming back.

Sometimes, God will direct us to do unusual things. My advice to you would be to never question His leading and always do what He says. My Bible still says this in John 10:27 "My sheep hear my voice, and I know them, and they follow me". Don't ever question His leading because He will never lead you astray. Pay it forward and God will bless in ways we never imagined.

Scriptures For This Chapter

Ecclesiastes 11:1 "Last thy bread upon the waters: for thou shalt find it after many days."

John 10:27 "My sheep hear my voice, and I know them, and they follow me."

Chapter 12

Getting a Big Surprise While Driving Home One Night

For anyone who knows me well, you understand that I'm a big believer in sowing and reaping. Any time a human being sows seeds, whether good or evil, you can mark it down that seed is coming back later down life's road. The Word of God teaches in Galatians 6:7-8 "That whatsoever a man soweth that shall he also reap". Always be aware of this verse in all decisions that you make. If you want to have a life that is blessed by the hand of Almighty God, make it a habit every day to sow good seeds. Sometimes things we sow in faith during our younger years will spring up in a great fashion years down the road. This next story is an example of that and I pray it encourages you to sow good seeds towards others.

When I was a young man at Open Door Baptist Church, my life was consumed in helping other ministries. Nothing in the world meant more to me than helping some ministry reach its full potential. My heart was fixed on God and every check was gladly going towards the Gospel of Jesus Christ. When I reflect back on those years, great joy fills my soul because I know treasures have been laid up in Heaven and no one can take that away from me. Jesus instructed us in Matthew 6:20 to "Lay up treasures in Heaven" and we will never regret it. When you lay up treasures in Heaven and help others along life's journey, great things will be in your future and God will return the favor. God promises us that if we sow good seeds, we will never go without and He will raise up people to bless us and what I'm about to tell you will prove just that. One night while driving down the road I noticed I was being followed by a vehicle and it lasted all the way until I got home. When I pulled into my driveway, this man pulled right behind me and got out of his car. Honestly, I was a little nervous because I had no idea who it was so I allowed him to approach my vehicle. When the man got to my car, I noticed it was a big man so I reached for any weapon available to defend myself. As I rolled down the window, I quickly noticed that it was a dear brother that I hadn't seen for a long time. This great man told me that from out of nowhere God convicted him about bringing me some money to be a blessing so he followed me to give it to me. He said "Brother, I'm doing this because 10 years ago you helped my family when I was in need so I'm doing the same thing for you". He said "Tony, hold out your hand". So I listened to the man of God. When I reached out my hand he placed $390 in it and he said "I love you Bro". Folks, every time we sow good seeds, God in Heaven takes records. We really needed that money and God's timing was perfect once again.

I want to encourage you to trust God and invest in others and I promise God will respond in a great way. The

Bible says in Psalm 18:25 "With the merciful thou wilt show thyself merciful". Give it a try everyone and see what God can do.

Scriptures For This Chapter

Psalm 18:25 "With the merciful thou wilt show thyself merciful; with an upright man thou wilt show thyself upright."

Galatians 6:8 "For he that soweth to his flesh shall of the flesh reap corruption; but he that soweth to the spirit shall of the spirit reap life everlasting."

Matthew 6:20 "But lay up for yourselves treasures in Heaven, where neither moth nor rust doth corrupt, and where thieves do not break through nor steal."

Chapter 13

Our God Knows What We Have Need Of

So often when the storms of life gather, and the pressures of life flood our soul, we have a tendency to focus on the storm instead of the Savior. When hard times arise and bills come to our mailbox, sadly we allow worry to distress us and fear to grip our hearts. As Christians, we must understand that we serve a God that knows the future and He understands exactly what we are going through. Although we may experience emotions and feelings that feel out of our control, let me remind you that God is not stressed out and He has everything under control. Many times throughout life God has a clear reason why He does things but we as humans cannot see the future so we immediately turn to doubt instead of trust. The Bible says in II Timothy 1:7 "For God hath not given us the spirit of fear; but of power, and of love, and of a sound mind". The Bible also says in I John 4:18 "But perfect love casteth out fear". We as children of God have the victory and may I remind you that I John 5:4 says "and this is the victory that overcometh the world, even our faith". God does not want us to live a life of fear but rather a life of faith, love, and confidence in what He can do through us if we will trust Him. Psalm 62:8 tells us to "trust Him at all times". The Lord is not in Heaven stressing out about our situations like we are and He has a reason for everything He does in our lives. God desires for us to seek His face when problems come, and if we do, great things will happen. The next story will be a blessing to you as it was for us.

    A short time ago my wife and I received two different bills in the mail that arrived unexpectedly that totaled $503. My wife looked at me and said "What are we going to do about these bills? What should we do?" My response to Erin was "I don't want to have to borrow the money, but we may have to". Once I made this statement God's spirit showed up and reminded me that prayer is always the answer so I decided to pray about $503 coming in. The Bible says in Jeremiah 33:3 "Call unto me, and I will answer thee, and show thee great and mighty things, which though knowest not" so I clung unto that verse for a few days. When Sunday arrived, a dear woman approached me and said "Tony, God wants me to give you $75, I hope it's a blessing". The gift that the woman gave me was a blessing and I began to seek His face again, trusting Him for the rest of the money. We went home, had a great afternoon, and before church I approached the Throne Room of Grace one final time, trusting that the money would come in. We went back to church, heard some great preaching, and as we went to leave a man of God had a gift he wanted to give us. This man told my wife that God had been dealing with him about giving us some money and he handed my wife a huge pile of cash that she just put in her purse. When we got home, we counted it together and to our amazement it was $432. All in all that day, between the $75 and the $432, our bills were paid with $5 to spare. There is a great lesson we learned from this moment in time, and that is to always make God the first option and things will always turn out right. Let me close this chapter out with Hebrews 4:16 "Let us therefore come boldly unto the Throne of Grace, that we may obtain mercy, and find grace to help in time of need".

Scriptures For This Chapter

Psalm 62:8 "Trust in Him at all times; ye people, pour out your heart before Him: God is a refuge for us. Selah."

Jeremiah 33:3 "Call unto me, and I will answer thee, and show thee great and mighty things, which thou knowest not."

II Timothy 1:7 "For God hath not given us the spirit of fear; but of power, and of love, and of a sound mind."

I John 4:18 "There is not fear in love; but perfect love casteth out fear: because fear hath torment. He that feareth is not made perfect in love."

I John 5:4 "For whatsoever is born of God overcometh the world: and this is the victory that overcometh the world, even our faith."

Chapter 14

There's a Miracle in the Making

When Jesus Christ walked among the crowds during His earthly ministry, people from every walk of life tried to get near Him. Jesus' fame increased more and more with each passing day and that caused many people who were sick and in pain to hunger and thirst after His healing touch even more. The four Gospels are loaded with many different stories of men and women who got to the point of getting completely desperate for a miracle and they clearly knew Jesus was exactly what they needed. Men and women from every country were doing whatever it took to get to Jesus and whenever folks had this mindset, Jesus would have compassion on them and heal them. We as Christians in this day and age need to take a page out of their book and hunger again after healing from the Master. As long as people hold onto their problems and refuse to seek after God, they will remain in their broken state of life; void of any help from on high. When we know we need help, we must swallow our pride and do whatever it takes to draw near to the hem of His garment. Jesus is looking to perform miracles in all of our lives, but it will never happen without brokenness and a hunger for healing. I never want to get to the point where my lack of faith or pride holds back miracles in my life. Every day we should seek the Lord at a deeper level and long for that touch from above. We serve a God of the supernatural and the only thing that limits His power is our lack of faith towards Him. The next story will highlight the ability God has to perform miracles in our lives if we just believe he can. Allow this story to speak to your heart.

Not long ago, the precious Savior opened up a door to get my book Walking On The Water With Jesus to some billionaires from Texas, but I literally had no money to even pay for the shipping costs. A dear woman told me that if I sent the book, she would personally take it to them so I immediately tried to figure out a way to make this happen. I recall sitting down at work and pulling up a song on YouTube called "There's A Miracle In The Making" and the words really began to do wonders for me. Over and over again I replayed that song and really tried to take in the words. On the fourth time of listening to that song, a peace like a dove swept over my soul and I knew my miracle was on the way. After I was done listening to this great song God gave me joy unspeakeable that remained for the remainder of that day. Moments later while walking down the road picking up trash a car came towards me at a high speed and stopped right beside me. The window rolled down and a dear lady started throwing money at me under Holy Ghost conviction. The dear woman looked at me and said "While I was sitting at home, God told me very clearly to come up to the school and give you $100 so you must take it". Directly after making this remark, she drove off saying "God Bless You". When my work day was over, I immediately sent a book to the billionaires and now we are friends on Facebook. God is able to perform miracles for all of us but we must believe He can and will. Matthew 15:28 says it like this "Then Jesus answered and said unto her, o woman, great is thy faith: be it unto thee even as thou wilt, and her daughter was made whole from that very hour". Praise God for faith, mercy, and His everlasting compassion towards them that believe He can do the impossible. Let's end this chapter with this great verse Matthew 19:26 "But Jesus beheld them, and said unto them, with men this is impossible: but with God all things are possible".

Scriptures For This Chapter

Matthew 15:28 "Then Jesus answered and said unto her, O woman, great is thy faith: be it unto thee even as thou wilt. And her daughter was made whole from that very hour."

Matthew 19:26 "But Jesus beheld them, and said unto them, with men this is impossible; but with God all things are possible."

Chapter 15

Jesus Is Always There When We Need Him

One of my favorite passages in the Bible is found in Isaiah 43:2. This wonderful verse is an encouragement to me and it has been an encouragement to millions down through the years. Whenever you feel down in spirit, run to this verse and verses like it for the comfort that you need. Isaiah 43:2 reads like this "When thou passeth through the waters, I will be with thee; and through the rivers, they shall not overflow thee: when thou walkest through the fire, thou shalt not be burned; neither shall the flame kindle upon thee". According to this verse, no matter how alone we feel, God will be near us. No matter what storm we are encountering, God has promised to walk through the fire with us. Child of God, we are never alone and never allow Satan to convince you that you are. The Devil loves to work overtime to discourage us, but God works overtime to enhance our faith and He uses verses like Isaiah 43:2 to accomplish this in our life. Always trust the purity of God's voice over the lies of the wicked one. Whenever you are going through a battle, understand that your feelings and emotions will try to take over. When this happens, slow yourself down and eliminate your fear by running to the truths from the Word of God. This next story will be a blessing to all of us who feel overwhelmed by the pressures of life. We have a God that wants to help and if you run to Him, He will hear your cry for help. Allow this following story to minister to your soul.

Not long ago on a Tuesday morning at around 7:15 A.M. I received a message from a dear friend of mine and right away I could tell he needed prayer. This wonderful brother started to desire prayer for his finances and he has never been one to ask before. This man has always been a blessing, so immediately I started to pray for my friend. I remember bowing my head right there on the spot and asking God to open up Heaven for this saint and to do something unusual as only He can. When I lifted up my head a peace came over me and a sweet verse swept over my soul. The verse that flooded my soul was Psalm 46:1 which says "God is our refuge and strength, a very present help in trouble". After thinking over this verse for a few minutes, I felt led to go inside the school I was working at and I could feel my steps being ordered by the Lord. When I was walking through the building a woman named Honey stopped me and her news was glorious. She said "Tony, I thought of you this morning and wanted to ask you if you had a need for some free cereal". I looked at her and said "Sure, I have a friend I just prayed for and he needs help". She said "You can have as much as you need". Folks, I walked away with full boxes of mini cereals. Each box contained 96 boxes in it and in total I was able to give this man I prayed for 576 boxes of cocoa puffs for his family to enjoy. After this took place, I looked up into Heaven and said "Yes Lord, that was unusual and I praise you for it". My friends, life may get rough and hope may seem to vanish from view, but I assure you that God has not gone out of business and He loves you very much. We serve a supernatural God. Psalm 46:10 says "Be still and know that I am God. Amen and Amen. O taste and see that the Lord is good".

Scriptures For This Chapter

Psalm 46:1 "God is our refuge and strength, a very present help in trouble."

Psalm 46:10 "Be still, and know that I am God: I will be exalted among the heathen, I will be exalted in the earth."

Psalm 34:8 "O taste and see that the Lord is good: blessed is the man that trusteth in Him."

Isaiah 43:2 "When thou passest through the waters, I will be with thee: and through the rivers, they shall not overflow thee: when thou walkest through the fire, thou shalt not be burned; neither shall the flame kindle upon thee."

Malachi 3:10 "Bring ye all the tithes into the store house, that there may be meat in mine house, and prove me now herewith, saith the Lord of hosts, if I will not open you the windows of heaven, and pour you out a blessing, that there shall not be room enough to receive it."

Chapter 16

The Lord Will Hear When I Call Upon Him

No matter how great the need is, God can meet that need through the avenue of prayer. Jesus declared in Matthew 7:7 "Ask, and it shall be given to you; seek, and ye shall find; knock, and it shall be opened unto you". Jesus also made the statement in Matthew 21:22 "And all things, whatsoever ye shall ask in prayer, believing, ye shall receive". James 4:2 says clearly "Yet ye have not, because ye ask not". Hebrews 4:16 plainly says "Let us come boldly unto the Throne Room of Grace, that we may obtain mercy, and find grace to help in time of need". The Bible teaches that God has all the answers, and without coming to Him through prayer in total faith, we will remain hopeless and searching for the truth. Jesus said in John 14:6 that "I am the way, the truth, and the life, and no man cometh unto the father, but by me". The quicker we understand that God has what we need, the better off we will be. The Lord is the great problem solver, the great burden bearer, and the greatest friend one could ever have. Proverbs 18:24 says "There is a friend that sticketh closer than a brother". Matthew 11:28 says "Come unto me, all ye that labor and are heavy laden, and I will give you rest". People all around this world are tired and weary and little do they know that Jesus has His arms open wide to any and all who will come unto Him. When I find myself in a mess and I don't know what to do, I find myself going to Jesus and I always leave satisfied with that choice. As the famous song says, "Give Up and Let Jesus Take Over". The next story is an example of the benefits of asking God for help and allowing Him to come through. I pray this story will bless you.

One day as I was alone at home, I had a burden heavy on my heart that was weighing me down. After about 10 minutes of trying to figure it out on my own the sweet Holy Spirit whispered in my ear "Why don't you allow me to help?" When I heard this still small voice, I dropped to my knees and said this prayer "Lord, you know this need, please help me if you will". Moments later, there was a knock at my door so I went to answer it. When I opened the door a sweet lady handed me flowers for my wife and a check for $200. As she left that day, a great burden had lifted from my soul, and I wondered why I didn't do that sooner. If you have a burden weighing you down, don't delay, run to Jesus today. Revelation 3:20 says "Behold, I stand at the door, and knock: if any man hear my voice, and open the door, I will come in to Him, and will sup with Him, and He with me".

Scriptures For This Chapter

Proverbs 18:24 "A man that hath friends must show himself friendly: and there is a friend that sticketh closer than a brother."

Matthew 7:7 "Ask, and it shall be given unto you; seek, and ye shall find; knock, and it shall be opened unto you."

Matthew 11:28 "Come unto me, all ye that labor and are heavy laden, and I will give you rest."

Matthew 21:22 "And all things, whatsoever ye shall ask in prayer, believing, ye shall receive."

John 14:6 "Jesus saith unto him, I am the way, the truth, and the life: no man cometh unto the father, but by me."

Hebrews 4:16 "Let us therefore come boldly unto the Throne of Grace; that we may obtain mercy, and find grace to help in time of need."

James 4:2 "Ye lust, and have not: ye kill, and desire to have, and cannot obtain: ye fight and war, yet ye have not, because ye ask not."

Revelation 3:20 "Behold, I stand at the door, and knock: if any man hear my voice, and open the door, I will come in to Him, and will sup with Him, and He with me."

Chapter 17

Call Unto Me and I Will Answer Thee

God in Heaven desires to answer our prayers, but only if we approach Him with a clean heart. David said in Psalm 66:18 "If I regard iniquity in my heart, the Lord will not hear me". The reason we cannot seem to get prayers to go past the ceiling is because we know deep in our hearts that something we are doing is grieving the spirit of God. It is not that God can't answer our prayers, but it's because God refuses to answer our prayers because our sin is standing in the way. Isaiah 59:2 says "But your iniquities have separated between you and your God". People all around this planet refuse to come clean with God and it results in a dead prayer life. Life is too short and God is too good for Christians to live in that way. If Christians would just worry more about impressing God rather than impressing man, our churches could experience revival once again. In Acts 4:31 we read a powerful account of men who had clean lives and could get a hold of God. Acts 4:31 says that "When they had prayed, the place was shaken where they were assembled together; and they were all filled with the Holy

Ghost". Folks, this is what we desperately need again, people that hunger and thirst for the power of God who can pray in the Holy Ghost like Jude talked out. God has not and will not change and He never will. Sadly, we are the ones who changed and it breaks God's heart. The Bible still says that God is able to do exceeding abundantly above all that we can ask or think. This next story will once again prove that God is still on the throne and He still answers prayer.

    Not long ago, I received a text message from a Godly sweet lady that really blessed my heart. In the message, this woman made it clear that she felt God wanted her to give me $60 just to be a blessing and it touched my heart. As fast as I could, I sent her a text back saying that I believe God would give this woman five times the amount she gave me and that I was trusting it would happen. Later that night, the school was having a carnival and they were raffling off prizes worth a lot of money. There were hundreds and hundreds of people there that night, trying to win the prizes that were available. When the numbers were called, this dear precious saint had a winning number and walked away with one of the prizes and it happened to be worth five times the amount she gave me. You see, folks, the power is there, we just are not tapping into it. Elijah prayed just 63 words and the fire of God fell. It's not the length of the prayer that carries the most weight, it's the purity of our hearts that does. Come clean with God and you too can make this statement "In my distress, I called upon the Lord and cried unto my God: He heard my voice out of His temple, and my cry came before Him, even into His ears". God is still able to hear and answer any prayer we have, but we must humbly seek His face in order for this to happen.

Scriptures For This Chapter

Psalm 18:6 "In my distress I called upon the Lord, and cried unto my God: He heard my voice out of His temple, and my cry came before Him, even into His ears."

Psalm 66:18 "If I regard iniquity in my heart, the Lord will not hear me."

Isaiah 59:2 "But your iniquities have separated between you and your God, and your sins have hid His face from you, that He will not hear."

Acts 4:31 "And when they had prayed, the place was shaken where they were assembled together; and they were all filled with the Holy Ghost, and they spoke the Word of God with boldness."

Ephesians 3:20 "Now unto Him that is able to do exceeding abundantly above all that we ask or think, according to the power that worketh in us."

Jude 1:20 "But ye beloved, building up yourselves on your most holy faith, praying in the Holy Ghost."

Chapter 18

The Goodness of God Leadeth Thee to Repentance

The Word of God clearly teaches in Psalm 33:5 that the earth is full of the goodness of the Lord. Folks, there could never be a more truthful statement than that. The goodness of God is overwhelming at times and it should bring us to our knees in total gratitude and worship for what He has done and for what He is doing for us all. The goodness of God ought to lead everyone on Earth to repentance. Psalm 145:2 says that "Every day will I bless thee: and I will praise thy name forever and ever". Psalm 145:8 says that "The Lord is gracious, and full of compassion: slow to anger, and of great mercy". Psalm 34:1 says it like this "I will bless the Lord at all times: His praise shall continually be in my mouth". Psalm 150:6 says "Let everything that hath breath praise the lord. Praise ye the Lord". Far too many Christians fail to notice and fail to focus on God's goodness and it really hampers and effects the way they live. Always remember this verse as you live your daily life: Romans 8:6 says "For to be carnally minded is death; but to be spiritually minded is life and peace". In other words, if you train your mind to be negative, you will always fail as a Christian. However, on the flipside, if you train yourself to think positive, life and peace will always be close by. The Bible still says it like this "And we know that all things work together for good to them that love God, to them who are the called according to His purpose". Every single morning we get out of bed we should allow ourselves to enjoy life, enjoy creation, laugh, love, and walk with God as He has intended us to. We serve a God of love and a God of mercy. The Lord has showered down His blessings on every single one of us and he desires to work on us and conform us into the image of His dear son. Every day I walk planet Earth I want to notice the beauty of creation. I want to bask in the sunshine of His love. I want to cherish every precious moment and live a life that brings honor to His holy name. We are all here for a divine reason and we must sow as many good seed as we can, so later on in life fruit may burst forth because of it. We are bought with a price and we owe Him everything. Whenever we sow good seeds you can mark it down that seed is coming back towards us in the same fashion every time. The following story will prove this is true and it will also show us what a good God we serve.

    Many years ago, on a Wednesday night, God suddenly started to convict me about selling my car and giving it to a preacher. Without any hesitation, I surrendered to His voice and gave the preacher my car while knowing that somewhere down the road God would remember this decision and bless me for it. Galatians 6:7 says "For whatsoever a man soweth that shall he also reap" and I've always believed every word of it because God cannot and will not lie. Folks, years went by and nothing ever happened, but God was working behind the scenes on our behalf. One day, my wife made a statement that maybe we shouldn't have given that car away and maybe we should have sold it and paid off some bills. I remember turning to her and saying "Honey, we made the right decision, and God always honors giving and He always returns the favor". Two weeks later, I got a call from my wife that her grandfather felt led to give us his 2007 impala with just 57,000 miles on it. We are still driving this car today, and it is such a blessing.

James 1:17 says that "Every good gift and every perfect gift cometh from above". Every step we take, every move we make, and every gift we enjoy, all comes from the hand of God. We all should realize that our God is good and He works on our behalf on a daily basis. Psalm 68:19 says "Daily the Lord loadeth us up with benefits". It's high time we understand that God is good to all and He is worthy of all praise. Every time we sow good seeds He in return will bless us in the same way, somewhere down life's road. This story is just proof of that statement, and I could give you hundreds more like it. God's goodness is such a beautiful thing.

Scriptures For This Chapter

Psalm 33:5 "He loveth righteousness and judgement: the earth is full of the goodness of the Lord."

Psalm 34:1 "I will bless the Lord at all times: His praise shall continually be in my mouth."

Psalm 145:2 "Every day will I bless thee; and I will praise thy name for ever and ever."

Psalm 68:19 "Blessed be the Lord who loadeth us up with benefits, even the God of our salvation. Selah."

Psalm 145:8 "The Lord is gracious, and full of compassion; slow to anger, and of great mercy."

Psalm 150:6 "Let everything that hath breath praise the Lord. Praise ye the Lord."

Romans 2:4 "Or despisest thou the riches of His goodness and forbearance and long-suffering; not knowing that the goodness of God leadeth thee to repentance?"

Romans 8:6 "For to be carnally minded is death; but to be spiritually minded is life and peace."

Romans 8:28 "And we know that all things work together for good to them that love God, to them who are the called according to His purpose.

Titus 1:2 "In hope of eternal life, which God, that cannot lie, promised before the world began;"

Galatians 6:7 "Be not deceived; God is not mocked: for whatsoever a man soweth, that shall he also reap."

James 1:17 "Every good gift and every perfect gift is from above, and cometh down from the Father of Lights, with whom is no variableness, neither shadow of turning."

Chapter 19

But My God Shall Supply All Your Need

It never ceases to amaze me how God Almighty supplies every need of His children. Time would not permit me to dive into the many stories I've seen through the years concerning this subject. Over and over again, I've watched God bring people to the very limits of their faith only to watch Him step in on His perfect timetable and supply their every need. We serve the God of all power and understanding and we must learn to trust Him no matter how dark our situation may be. By the authority of God's holy word, we can have complete faith that God will come through when we need Him most and He knows exactly what we have need of. There is a quote that helps me so often throughout my life and it helps remind me of the faithfulness of God. This quote is very simple and very profound: "Always trust God's promises that never change over your feelings that change all throughout the day". If we can rest in the fact that the Bible is a solid rock and our feelings are shifting sand, we can stand any raging storm that comes our way. This next story will be just another example of God's mercy in the area of Him supplying every need, whether big or small.

One day, as we were all sitting around eating dinner, my wife said "Honey, isn't it time to get some new shoes?" When she said this, I looked down at my shoes, which looked like they had been through the war, and I knew it was time to consider buying new shoes. My wife said "Let's go to Walmart and get some new shoes" and I said "Alright, we will after dinner". Directly after marking this statement, God started dealing with me about waiting a while and trusting Him so we cancelled our trip to Walmart. The very next day while working at Huron High School, a woman approached me with some wonderful news that blessed my soul. In her hands were red Nike Air shoes and she said "Tony, you were the first one to come to my mind, do you need some shoes?" My response to her was "Yes, what size are they?" She responded by saying they were size 11 and that happened to be my exact size. When she handed me the shoes, I just knew that was an answer to prayer and that God made that happen. God loves to provide for His own and what's even more amazing about this story is the fact that two more pairs of shoes were given to me that same day, and they also were size 11. We serve a loving God that knows what we need before we even ask. Rest in the fact that God will come through every time we place our trust in Him. My Bible still says "But my God shall supply all your need according to His riches in glory by Christ, Jesus". If the blessed holy book says it just believe it, don't doubt it. Always remember that the just shall live by the faith and there is no other way to live if we want to please him.

Scriptures For This Chapter

Philippians 4:19 "But my God shall supply all your need according to His riches in glory by Christ, Jesus."

Romans 1:17 "For therein is the righteousness of God revealed from faith to faith: as it is written, the just shall live by faith."

Chapter 20

Amazing Grace, How Sweet the Sound

The greatest song every written was penned by one of the worst infidels that has ever lived. The song is Amazing Grace, and the man was John Newton. This song displays the love of God that can reach the vilest of sinners. John Newton invented new curse words, and went to any extreme to rebel against the teachings of his Godly mother. Mr. Newton would drink, smoke, cuss God, steal, lie, cheat, abuse, slander, and run around and laugh at Holy living. He owned slaves, and by his own words was capable of anything. At his lowest point in life, God sent a violent storm his way when he was travelling by way of ship one night. The storm was so fierce that it forced Mr. Newton to realize that he may die, and he knew he was unprepared to meet his maker. Suddenly, versus flooded back to his memory that his mother taught him when he was a child. Deep conviction struck his heart and in the midst of the storm he began to seek after God like never before. The Lord heard his cry, and Mr. John Newton was transformed in a supernatural way. The God he hated was the God he suddenly adored. The song Amazing Grace is his personal testimony of how wonderful the grace of God was for him, and can be for you if you would only receive it. This song as reached the masses for Christ, and has become almost bigger than life.

For the rest of this chapter, I would like to borrow the third verse of this wonderful hymn and apply it to my own life. You will see the mercy and grace of God in the way of divine protection and safety towards me in a breathtaking fashion. God has watched over my life, and sent His angels to protect me over and over again. The third verse of the song Amazing Grace reads like this: "Through many dangers, toils, and snares, I have already come, thus grace has brought me safe thus far, and grace will lead me home". In the next few minutes, I will give you a brief description of many close calls that I have had, and I will show God's hand of safety through all of them. Paul once gave a list in II Corinthians 11:23-28 and showed God's watchful care during His ministry, and that's what I aim to do in this chapter. My desire is to magnify God through these stories, and reveal the fact that He is the potter and I am the clay. Let me start from my beginning and slowly go through my life, bragging on the grace of God.

It all started when my mother was carrying me in her womb. She told me how she was riding a bike one day and fell off that bike on her belly, exactly where my head was located. She told me how she went to the doctors and told them what had took place. The doctors feared that there could be brain damage due to her fall and it was something to be concerned with. Through prayer and God's grace, I turned out fine and my parents thank God for it to this day. Another problem I faced upon being born was a very rare back problem. There was a step in my spine that only 50 people in America had at the time. This problem crippled most who had it, and the situation was very serious. My problem was placed on the prayer list, and within 3 days my back was healed.

When I was around 7 years old, I almost drowned, before my mother saved me. As a child, I remember stepping on some old nasty glass one day that cut my foot wide open and there was blood everywhere. This could have caused disease and infection, but praise God, my foot is fine today. While playing baseball in the yard one day my brother hit a baseball around 100 miles per hour and hit me in the face from about 35 feet away. This could have killed me if it would have been hit just right, but I shook it off and kept playing. Another scary moment took place when my mom hit a deer at around 45 miles per hour and severely damaged her van. My brother Bobby and I were in the van, but walked away with no injury to show for it. I remember while golfing one day as a teenager, on the ninth hole of a course called Harbor Club, lightening hit a tree next to me. At the time when it struck the tree, I had a metal club in my hand.

Another scary incident happened while working on the road one afternoon, driving signs into the ground with a 75 pound jack hammer. I was holding stubs in place while another man used the jack hammer to drive them into the ground. This jack hammer could drive through concrete and was very powerful. As we were working, my hand was too high on the stub, and the man I was working with put the jackhammer right on my thumb and started driving the stub with my thumb caught under it for over 4 seconds before he noticed. The pain was beyond anything I had ever experienced, but I kept my finger, and it has healed up now. Praise God, he spared my finger, and I'm glad it wasn't much worse than it was. I fell off a truck one day, from about 12 feet in the air, and landed on my tail bone. Although it hurt, nothing broke, and I was okay.

One day while working on the freeway, a car crossed the yellow line and almost ran over my foot. Another time at work, the wind caught 14 signs and I found myself under them. Each sign was 108 pounds apiece; totaling over 1400 pounds that fell on me. I should be paralyzed, but I'm still waking fine today, and I returned to work 2 days later.

When you look at my life, I'm almost like a walking miracle.

Many years ago when I was working in Ohio, something happened very early in the morning that woke me up pretty quick. I was setting barrels out to close traffic when, from out of nowhere, a semi-truck took a barrel out of my hand, and took it up the road about half a mile. If I would not have let go of that barrel, I probably would have lost my hand.

To say I've been lucky just isn't good enough, I believe God's hand has protected me all these years.

I still remember the day I was part of a six car accident on Southfield Freeway with multiple spinouts involved. The sight was almost like watching a movie, with all the sights and sounds it produced. No one was seriously hurt, and I was praising God. Another incident that comes to mind is when I fell asleep at the wheel at 3:00 in the morning and almost tipped my S-10 pickup over at 70 miles per hour. God kept me safe and kept that from happening. I also remember getting lost while driving one day and heading towards oncoming traffic. Thank God somehow I avoided an accident, and was able to make it safely to my destination.

Time after time, day after day, God's hand seems to guide me around pitfalls and dangers in my life. Please allow me to give you a few more examples of close calls.

One day while driving in the winter time, I hit black ice and spun out of control. When it was all said and done, I ended up landing in a ditch, face down, a foot from a tree on one side, and 2 feet from a mailbox on the other. My truck was badly damaged, but I was safe and sound. Something else that comes to mind is the time my tire blew out, heading to Cedar Point, and my truck went across lines of traffic, almost hitting cars. It was almost like landing a plane, but after it was over, once again I was safe. A few years back, my car died in a busy intersection and a number of cars almost hit me head on, and if so I would probably be in bad shape today. While playing football one day, I was tossed in the air and landed on my neck. After a few minutes of sitting out of the game, I returned without injury. At a greenhouse one day, while closing an old glass window, I was severely cut on the head and bled for over an hour. I returned to work the next day. Around a month later, at the same greenhouse, my lip was cut open this time, and I bled for around 2 hours.

I have almost been shot twice, been hit by cars, been in more accidents and close calls then I can count. I've almost hit a few deer crossing the road, and nearly got on a ride at Cedar Point in which a man died on 5 minutes later. The list goes on and on, and the fact is, I really should be dead right now. David said it perfectly when he said "There is but a step between me and death". The Bible tells us in Psalms 34:7 that "The angels of God encampeth around them that fear Him". God has sheltered and protected me, and I am forever in debt for His grace in my life. I took a list at home and counted around 43 times where I could have died or been crippled but Gods mercy protected me. The song Amazing Grace is more than just a song, it is a biblical reality. My life has been nothing short of amazing, and his hand of protection has lead me every step of the way. Like Fanny Crosby once wrote "To God be the glory, great things He hath done". The Bible says in Psalms 34:19 that many are the afflictions of the righteous; but the Lord delivereth him out of them all". God deserves all the praise for everything He does, and I hope through this chapter we have seen this. The fourth verse of Amazing Grace reads like this "When we've been there ten thousand years, bright shining as the sun, we've known less days to sing God's praise than when we first begun". Let's end this chapter with Psalm 23:4 "Yea, though I walk through the valley of the shadow of death, I will fear no evil: for thou art with me: thy rod and thy staff they comfort me. Amen and Amen."

Scriptures For This Chapter

Psalm 23:4 "Yea though I walk through the valley of the shadow of death, I will fear no evil; for thou art with me: thy rod and thy staff they comfort me."

Psalm 34:19 "Many are the afflictions of the righteous: but the Lord delivereth Him out of them all."

CONCLUSION

As we conclude this book I want to sincerely thank you all for taking the time to read this feeble effort for the Lord. Lord willing, the stories contained in this book touched your soul and blessed you in various ways. Folks, we serve a supernatural God of mercy who displays His love to mankind on a continual basis. We that know Christ are bought with a price and, if the truth be told, we owe Him everything. We as Christians need to surrender all to the Lord and serve Him with every fiber of our being.

My prayer for this book is that in the years to come, when folks read these stories, it will drive them to the very throne room of God. We need people on the front line for God again, sold out to further the cause of Christ. This world needs us to be the salt of the earth and the light of the world again. Folks, simply put, we need revival and that's my heart's desire. Soaring With Eagles Volume 2 is meant to infuse life and victory in the believer's life again and I pray it has and will in the future.

SOARING WITH EAGLES Volume 2

ANTHONY RITTHALER

www.ingramcontent.com/pod-product-compliance
Lightning Source LLC
Chambersburg PA
CBHW071750080526
44588CB00013B/2207